Contents

This booklet was produced in 2004, to celebrate 100 years since the ancient Collegiate Church of St Salvator became the official University Chapel.

Worship

Welcome from the Chaplain

Rev Dr James Walker

From whatever direction you arrive in St Andrews the tower of St Salvator's Chapel can be seen standing out above the rooftops. Just as distinctly, within the Chapel, you can begin to sense its unique contribution to the life of the University and the town.

Whether you come as a student or staff member, as an alumnus or visitor, we hope that, as you walk around, you will understand why the Chapel has inspired countless people ever since its foundation in 1450. We invite you to share in its on-going life of prayer, whether by taking time to sit and pray, enjoying its silence or its music, or by joining us in worship. Please take time to pray for others, for the University and the town, and to think of your own life in the light of God's welcoming love given to you and everyone in Jesus Christ.

Aerial view of St Salvator's Chapel, Tower and Quad

Services

$\mathscr{C}$ome to the morning service on any Sunday during term and enjoy the particular atmosphere of worship in the University Chapel. The style of service varies each week, to incorporate the customs of the diverse University and wider community who worship here. Those who come will hopefully recognise their own traditions on at least some Sundays in the choice of hymns or prayers or preacher.

Worshippers present a colourful scene, with arts and science undergraduate students in red gowns, divinity students and graduates in black gowns, and staff members in robes of various colours. At the start of the service, the University mace, bearing the figure of St Andrew, is carried in at the head of the academic procession, while people stand to honour and give thanks for the gift of learning.

The University Mace

Following the service is the famous Pier Walk, a centuries-old tradition. Its roots may lie in the practice of escorting a visiting preacher back to his boat, although later it may have come to honour the courage of John Honey, a student who heroically rescued five men from a shipwreck in St Andrews Bay on New Year's Day, 1800.

Daily morning prayers and fortnightly evensong or vespers are held during term. Special annual services celebrate religious, University and town events, such as Christmas, Easter, Graduation, the commemoration of the town's martyrs, and the commemoration of those who have given their bodies for medical research. Those with a University connection can marry in the Chapel (right), and many former students return to St Andrews to do so, keen to celebrate their joy amid the scenes of their University days.

Music

The Chapel has a strong tradition of music, stretching back to the earliest students of St Salvator's College, who were expected to perform choral duties. Since the appointment of the first University organist in 1925, the St Salvator's Chapel Choir has become an increasingly important part of the University's music making. The current Choir, which numbers 45 members, sings at the Sunday services and the fortnightly evensong. The Choir also gives occasional concerts and undertakes a foreign tour every Easter. Other choirs, including the University's Renaissance group, which specialises in unaccompanied sacred music of the Renaissance period, perform occasionally in the Chapel.

History

The College of St Salvator

The University of St Andrews, founded between 1410 and 1414, is Scotland's oldest university. The College of St Salvator, now a part of the United College of St Salvator and St Leonard, is its earliest surviving college.

In its first days, although it had a clear structure and regulations, the University had no official buildings of its own. Masters and students lodged in the town, and lectures took place wherever space could be obtained, often in the Priory and other religious buildings, or the masters' own rooms.

In 1419 the first academic building was erected with the foundation of the College of St John, on South Street where Parliament Hall now stands. In 1430 it was followed by the establishment of a Pedagogy, or School, for the use of the Faculty of Arts. However, neither institution provided a definite focus for University life. They had not been properly endowed, and the College proved short-lived, while the Pedagogy was divided by the disputes of its masters. The University was threatened by the decline of student numbers, as Scots students returned to Paris following the end of the Great Schism in the Papacy (a religious dispute which divided Europe) which had prevented them from studying there.

James Kennedy, Bishop of St Andrews and Chancellor of the University 1440-1465, became convinced that the only solution to the University's problems lay in the foundation of a new college, properly funded and organised. On 27 August 1450, he formally inaugurated the College of St Salvator, personally laying the four corner stones of the planned buildings on the site in North Street on which the College has remained to this day.

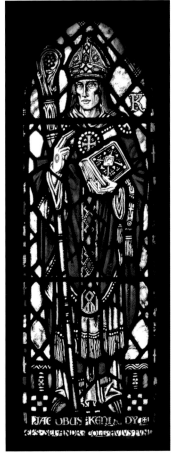

Kennedy believed that true learning and religion, the intellectual and spiritual life, were inseparable. The College of St Salvator, the Holy Saviour, was to be a college of Arts and Theology, established, as its Charter of Foundation states, for 'the praise of God, the strengthening of the Church, and the increase of the Christian religion.' Though numbers later greatly expanded, the founder members of the college comprised thirteen persons, in honour of Christ and the twelve Apostles. Naturally, the Collegiate Church lay at the heart of this splendid and ambitious foundation.

Bishop Kennedy window
in organ loft

The Collegiate Church of St Salvator: Mediaeval Interior

*T*he Church of St Salvator was consecrated in 1460, a mere ten years after building work had begun. It had a focal role in the life of the college: masters, who were in holy orders, and students, had specific religious duties. However from the outset the Church of St Salvator was intended to be more than a college chapel. It was a place where the services of the mediaeval church were celebrated with extraordinary magnificence and the Word of God was preached regularly to all people. It is notable that, unlike many college foundations, the main doors face outwards into the street rather than inwards to the quadrangle, inviting the people of St Andrews and beyond to come into the church.

In the mediaeval period, in order to serve its two roles as a public and a college church, the Church of St Salvator was divided by a screen separating the public nave in the west end from the collegiate choir in the east. In addition to the high altar, which would, as now, have been set in the eastern end in the centre of the apse, there were at least three lesser altars in the church. Those of St Mary the Virgin and St Michael were probably situated against the west side of the screen. There seem to have been five further altars beyond the church proper, such as that of St Katharine, which stood in a chapel on the north side. Attached to the various altars were chaplainries, often founded by private benefactors to celebrate masses for the souls of the patrons, their families and other named persons.

Inventories show the particular splendour with which the Church was furnished before the Reformation. The high altar was covered with, and surrounded by, richly embroidered fabrics such as blue velvet and cloth of gold. Upon it, at the centre of six silver candlesticks, stood a magnificent great gilt cross 'with ane crucifix Mare and John and the tuelf Apostolys.' A richly bound and enamelled gospel book was carried in before the ministers and placed on the altar.

Among the many other wonderful ornaments for the Church were a large silver image of Christ with a diadem or crown set with precious stones, silver gilt chalices for the celebration of mass and, perhaps most significant of all for the mediaeval congregation, an altar cross set with jewels, said to contain two pieces of the true cross. The overall effect of the splendid decoration was intended to be literally awe-inspiring.

St Salvator's Chapel and Tower

Window in organ loft depicting the martyrdom of Patrick Hamilton.

The Reformation Period

The turbulent religious period of the sixteenth century has left its marks on the Church of St Salvator. In 1528 Patrick Hamilton was burnt outside the college gates for his Protestant beliefs. Hamilton, whose reforming tendencies were encouraged by friends on the Continent, was accepted into the University's Faculty of Arts in 1524 and may have taught in the University for a short period. The initials PH on the cobbles below the church tower mark the site of his execution (right). Legend states that undergraduates who tread on them will fail their final examinations. The impression of a face on the tower above the initials is said to depict Hamilton and to have appeared miraculously to represent his martyrdom (see below).

On 1 March 1546 another Protestant reformer, George Wishart, was executed for heresy before St Andrews Castle. Following Wishart's death, Cardinal David Beaton, who had presided over his trial, was attacked and murdered in the Castle by a group of avengers including John Leslie, brother of the Earl of Rothes, his nephew Norman, and William Kirkcaldy of Grange. These men then took the Castle, which lies northeast of St Salvator's College. They, and supporters including John Knox, were besieged. A foray by the Protestant garrison in 1547 caused considerable fire-damage to the College. The timber spire of the Church, completed about 1530, was destroyed. The flat top was then used by the Catholic besiegers as a gun-emplacement for reducing the Castle, with shots being fired across the town. A stone spire was finally added in the 1550s; the parapet dates from about 1851.

During the Reformation, St Salvator's Church was stripped of its statues and much of its interior decoration, because they were thought to detract from the worship of God. From 1560 services within the Church ceased, as did the religious functions of the College envisaged by its founder. Like Kennedy, the reformers believed that learning and religion should be interlinked. However they felt that the members of a college should not stand apart but should join with their fellow-parishioners for worship and communion, in the case of St Salvator's College by attending the Town Kirk, Holy Trinity.

In 1563 the magistrates of St Andrews established the new Commissary Court (which replaced the pre-Reformation Church Court) within St Salvator's Church, somewhat to the dissatisfaction of the college masters who unsuccessfully attempted to evict them. Although the Church was occasionally used by Holy Trinity when its congregation became too large (particularly between 1598 and 1600), it was rarely employed for religious purposes for nearly two hundred years.

ollowing the Reformation, with no income from worshippers and college revenues reduced, the buildings of St Salvator's College lapsed into a semi-ruinous state. Although some attempt was made to improve the lecture rooms, dining hall and accommodation, the Church and cloister were apparently neglected. In 1633, Charles I received a report on the state of the University from the Archbishop of Canterbury, William Laud. He wrote to the Chancellor, Archbishop Spottiswoode, commenting that for University members to 'goe to the ordinarie Parish Church to service and sermone, and ther sitt promiscouslie with the rest of the auditorie . . . loses much of the honor and dignitie of the universitie.' He ordered that St Salvator's Church should be repaired and services resume there from 1634. However little, if anything, seems to have been done and the college members continued to attend Holy Trinity.

In 1681 Alexander Skene, Provost of St Salvator's College, petitioned the Privy Council for permission to organise a fund to restore the college buildings. The petition specifically mentioned the 'ruinous' state of the Church, and its steeple and cloister. Skene personally travelled throughout Scotland collecting donations. A remarkable £12,000 Scots was raised. Skene has been called the second founder of St Salvator's College, for his work arrested the decay of the buildings, in particular the Church, at a crucial time. He also re-cast the college bell and repaired the college mace. However, because of the University's support for the deposed James II / VII, Skene was removed from his post after the Revolution of 1688 (along with almost all the University staff), his work still incomplete.

Head and (opposite top) knop of the Mace of St Salvator's College

Within a generation, the college buildings had again fallen into disrepair, as various visitors' accounts reveal. John Macky, travelling round Scotland about 1723, wrote 'This College consists of two spacious Courts: Over the Gate is a very fine Stone Spire; and to the Right, as in the Colleges at Oxford, is a handsome Church or Chapel . . . and . . . a neat Cloister well pav'd and supported with Pillars; but neither it, nor the Church, so well preserv'd as in the Colleges of England, but seem rather entirely neglected.' He also noted that the 'Apartments for the Masters and Scholars' were 'unaccountably out of Repair, they being hardly at the Pains of keeping out Rain, or mending their Windows.' This may have been because the students, who were required to pay the college a deposit for damages which was rarely returned, were in the habit of smashing the windows at the end of the year to get their money's worth.

William Douglass (1728) admired the 'large vaulted Chapel' with its 'very high and lofty Spire.' He wrote: 'The common Hall and Schools are vastly large; and the Cloysters and Private Lodgings for Masters and Scholars have been very magnificent and convenient. The Fabrick is of late become very much out of repair, neither is the College Revenue able to support it.'

The University's three fifteenth-century maces.

The Union of the Colleges of St Salvator and St Leonard

By the mid-sixteenth century the University of St Andrews consisted of three colleges: St Salvator's, St Leonard's (founded 1512) and St Mary's (founded 1538). St Mary's was established on the site of the Pedagogy on South Street, and St Leonard's within the Priory precinct, near the Cathedral, where the private St Leonards School now stands. After the Reformation, in 1579, the Colleges of St Salvator and St Leonard were reconstituted as colleges of Arts and Philosophy, while the teaching of theology, once so important in all the colleges, was focused in St Mary's.

Arms of St Salvator's College

Declining student numbers and the poverty and decayed state of the buildings of the Arts colleges led to their union in 1747 as the United College of St Salvator and St Leonard. It was decided that the United College should be housed on the site of St Salvator's College, and after accommodation there had been rendered fit, St Leonard's College was abandoned. The buildings and gardens were sold off in 1772, with the exception of the College Church, the failing roof and tower of which were removed. St Leonard's Church had served the parish of St Leonard, as well as members of the college, and the congregation as a whole was transferred into the St Salvator's College loft in the Town Kirk in 1750.

Drawing by John Oliphant, about 1767, showing the shuttered windows.

Extensive renovations were undertaken at St Salvator's College, with much of the mediaeval fabric being destroyed. It was decided that St Salvator's Church, which was still partially occupied by the Commissary Court, should again be used for worship. Between 1759 and 1761 the roof was repaired, the floor relaid, new pews facing east installed, a western gallery built, a cross wall, which may have been the mediaeval screen, was removed, and the windows cleared of their mullions and tracery and given new wooden frames and shutters (see above).

In 1761, members of the United College and the parishioners of St Leonard transferred from Holy Trinity to St Salvator's Church and services were resumed. It was soon noticed that the great vaulted roof gave an unpleasant echo. Inspections raised concerns about its safety. James Craig, architect of Edinburgh's New Town, found that water had permeated the roof and into the walls, which were leaning due to the force exerted upon them. He recommended that the existing stone roof be replaced by one of timber and slate. During replacement, the old roof is said to have fallen into the Church, damaging Bishop Kennedy's tomb. The Church was re-seated and the gallery replaced.

Nineteenth Century Renovations

From 1820 the Common Tables, at which the students ate, were no longer maintained by the United College, and the residential system was abandoned. Student numbers had greatly increased, from just over 100 at certain points during the eighteenth century to about 200 by 1827, and it was no longer possible for the United College to provide accommodation for all the undergraduates. The complete cessation of the residential system marked a fundamental change to the structures established at the foundation of both St Salvator's and St Leonard's Colleges. The United College was not, as formerly, a home for an academic community of masters and students living together, but was instead a space in which teaching and learning took place, before those involved

United College Building Survey 1828 (Architect, Robert Reid)

went their separate ways. The Disruption of the Church of Scotland in 1843 brought further changes, with college members no longer obliged to worship in St Salvator's Church, but able to attend any church they wished. To meet its current needs the United College was extensively renovated between 1829 and 1849, with all the buildings except the church, tower, and block to the west of the church being replaced. In the mid-1840s, under the supervision of Hugh Lyon Playfair, Provost of St Andrews, various alterations were carried out to St Salvator's

Ceiling boss in ante-chapel

Church, including the removal of the shutters from the windows and the installation of new pews, a 'tastefully executed new pulpit' and gas lights. The existing cloister on the north side of the building was constructed under the architect William Nixon. Robert Matheson added a parapet and clock to the tower in about 1851.

In 1861 the Principal of the United College, James David Forbes, initiated a scheme to restore the Church to its full mediaeval splendour, partly to encourage college members to continue worshipping there. Matheson provided the designs, with the roof and seating being replaced and pinnacles added to the south front buttresses. The Church was further embellished in the Gothic Revivalist style, with the installation of an elaborate carved, traceried wooden screen, and tracery and stained glass for the windows. In 1864 the cloister was enclosed with glass screens to form a reading room for students. It also came to be used by the Debating Society and as a gymnasium, before once again being opened to the elements about 1930.

In 1900 Sir Robert Rowand Anderson designed a new pulpit for the Church, the design incorporating symbolism relating to the University. It was replaced in 1930 by the present sixteenth century pulpit. The Anderson pulpit is currently displayed in the Museum of Scotland, Edinburgh.

In the late nineteenth century there was a movement for St Salvator's Church to be occupied solely by the University. In 1904 a new church was erected at the west of St Andrews for the congregation of St Leonard's parish and on 16th October 1904 the ancient Collegiate Church of St Salvator became the official University Chapel.

The first part of the twentieth century saw a desire to refurbish the Church to modern standards, while retaining the integrity of its historical associations. The funds available were not sufficient to effect a full-scale refurbishment. However from 1921-22, under the architect Peter MacGregor Chalmers, the heating and lighting were replaced, the woodwork restored, and the plaster stripped from the walls to expose the original stonework. The sacristy door was uncovered and fitted with what may be the original door of the old college hall. The dais in the apse was paved with marble, the First World War memorial was erected and, slightly later, the marble communion table was installed.

An American benefactor, Edward Harkness, made possible the latest major refurbishment of the building. This was undertaken by the Scottish architect Reginald Fairlie, between 1929 and 1931.

Fairlie's scheme incorporates the stone screen supporting the wooden-fronted west gallery and the pews which face each other across the central aisle. He also constructed the vestry at the east end of the cloister.

Since this period, the only changes have been minor additions and alterations to the decoration.

Window in organ loft depicting Jubal, King David and Miriam.

Guided Tour

The Ante-Chapel

The ante-chapel contains various memorials, mainly to principals and professors of the University, though alumni are also represented, for example William Dalgleish Playfair (son of Hugh Lyon Playfair, Provost of St Andrews) killed in the Battle of Soobraon, India, in 1846.

Of particular interest is the tombstone of Provost Hugh Spens, who died in 1534, which provides the only known illustration of Scottish mediaeval academic dress.

The memorial to the writer and historian Andrew Lang is also notable. The Greek inscription was composed by his friend Dr Alexander Shewan and translates: 'A long farewell to thee, sea-washed seat of holy Andrew, pleasant to me in life and ever greatly longed for; and now art thou even dearer, little town, in that thou givest me, out-worn, eternal rest after toil.'

Three consecration crosses are engraved on the walls of the ante-chapel. There are various others throughout the Church: two can be seen on the west exterior wall and others are concealed behind panelling and in the tomb of Bishop Kennedy.

In a recess on the south wall, originally constructed as a tomb, are several fragments of sculpture, including representations of the Annunciation and Circumcision. These may once have formed part of the decoration of Bishop Kennedy's tomb.

Tombstone of Hugh Spens

The inscription on the screen is from 2 Corinthians 5:1. In translation it reads: 'For we know that if our earthly house of this tabernacle were dissolved, we have a building of God, a house not made with hands, eternal in the heavens.'

Consecration cross

The Nave and Apse

From the nave, the magnificent organ can be seen above the ante-chapel. The striking colour scheme is apparently intended to reflect the red gowns of the students and grey stones of St Andrews. It is the Chapel's third organ. The first, a late nineteenth century Willis instrument, went to the new St Leonard's Church in Hepburn Gardens, with the displaced congregation of St Leonard's parish. The second, another Willis instrument, was installed in 1904, and remained in service until 1973. The current organ was made by Gerhard Hradetzky and installed in 1974; it is widely regarded as one of the finest in Scotland. It is a four manual mechanical-action instrument in the classical style, containing just over 3,000 pipes.

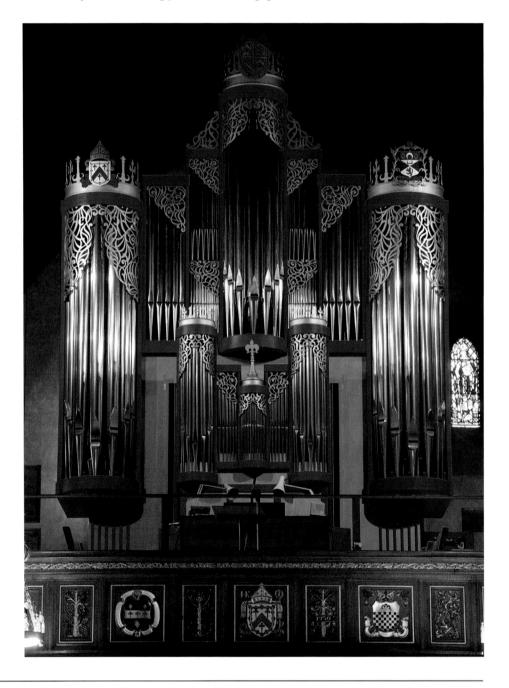

On the screen, in front of the organ loft, are the shields of the founders of the University of St Andrews and its colleges. That of Bishop Kennedy is in the centre, as befits his position as the founder of the Church. From left to right they are: Archbishop Hamilton, Archbishop Beaton and Cardinal Beaton, Bishop Wardlaw, Bishop Kennedy, Pope Benedict XIII, Archbishop Stewart and Prior Hepburn.

The roof of the church, with its traceried wooden braces and gilded band at the base, dates from Matheson's 1861 restoration. The exact function of the two small openings in the north wall is unclear. They may have lit a wall passage, which perhaps gave access to the mediaeval rood loft, or an apartment over the south cloister walk.

The Gothic-style pews are arranged 'choirwise' in tiers which run from east to west. The canopied stalls at the northeast are for the Principal and masters. The carvings represent the abundance of nature: note the birds, animals, fruit, flowers and foliage. On the upper pinnacle of the principal seat is an angel bearing the shield of the University. The elaborate design of this stall reflects the stonework of Kennedy's tomb. On the back of the stalls to the west of these, young angels play musical instruments. Carved animals also feature here: the dog is particularly attractive.

The pulpit dates from the late sixteenth century and originally belonged to Holy Trinity, the Town Kirk. It was brought to St Salvator's College in 1798 and installed here in 1930. The wrought-iron bracket would have held a sand-glass by which the minister could measure the length of his sermons, which were once expected to exceed two hours. Tradition says that this is the pulpit from which John Knox preached his rousing sermons in Holy Trinity, but it is probably of a slightly later date.

In the apse is the University's First World War memorial, installed under MacGregor Chalmers. The arcades of stonework bear the names of the fallen: the mosaics are by Douglas Strachan. Before the memorial is a marble communion table with a mosaic of the Last Supper, also designed by Strachan.

Communion Table

Bishop Kennedy's Tomb and the Sacrament House

The tomb of Bishop Kennedy lies close to the altar, on the north wall of the church. Though now badly damaged, it is splendidly carved and would once have presented a truly magnificent appearance. It was constructed during Kennedy's lifetime, probably by the Tournai School. The upper carved detail may represent Heaven as the 'House of Many Mansions' (John 14:2) or the Holy City in Revelation 21:2. The decorative elements are similar to those of the mace of St Salvator's College, commissioned by Bishop Kennedy and made in Paris in 1461 by John Maiel. To the left of the tomb is Kennedy's coat of arms (right).

The tomb has been opened on at least four occasions. During the 1842 excavation, under Robert Chambers, Kennedy's remains were examined. At this time, there was considerable interest in phrenology, the idea that a person's character is revealed through the shape of the head. Measurements were accordingly taken of Bishop Kennedy's skull, and it was determined that:

> 'this was the Head which, if containing a healthy brain, of good temperament, would denote a man of capacity and vigorous character. The perceptive organs were, however, better than the reflective; so that in point of high intellect, the Head was somewhat disappointing. Firmness was very large, and Cautiousness, Destructiveness, Adhesiveness, and Benevolence were all of super-average magnitude, pointing to a man of determined character, but generous disposition towards his fellow creatures.'

Bishop Kennedy's Tomb

A sceptic might say that sufficient was already known of Kennedy's life and works to reach this conclusion regarding his character.

The tomb was also opened in 1930, during restoration work on the building. Professor Waterston of the Anatomy Department examined Kennedy's bones, in the hope of determining information such as his age at death and evidence of disease. With the artist J T Murray he took detailed measurements of the skull and re-constructed Bishop Kennedy's appearance. The remains were then reinterred in a bronze casket and a short service held.

The Sacrament House, to the east of the tomb, was used to hold the Reserved Sacrament (the Bread, and occasionally also the Wine, consecrated at the Eucharist) and is the earliest datable example in Scotland. It consists of an aumbry (a recessed cupboard), below which two angels support a monstrance (a vessel used when exposing the consecrated Host for veneration). Above it are three shields. The left bears the royal arms of Scotland (for James II) and the right those of Bishop Kennedy. The centre shield has been erased, but probably bore the arms of Pope Pius II.

The Sacrament House

The Stained Glass

None of the original mediaeval glass survives: it seems to have been removed at the Reformation, when the Church was stripped of its furnishings. The windows were cleared of their mullions and tracery and given wooden shutters during the restoration of 1759-61. A drawing by John Oliphant, c1767 (page 15), shows the somewhat blinkered appearance these gave the Church.

The shutters remained in place until the mid-1840s, when they were removed and the windows fitted with clear glass. This was in turn replaced by stained glass during the refurbishment of the Church under Principal Forbes. Only two of the windows Forbes commissioned remain in the Church. The other windows were reglazed during the late nineteenth and twentieth centuries.

The three windows in the apse

The central window is a crucifixion scene, by Gordon Webster (1908-1987). To the left of the Cross are St Andrew, St Leonard and a figure who may be St John. At the foot are the three Marys. This window thus makes symbolic reference to all the patron saints of the town and University: St Andrew, with the Holy Saviour (St Salvator), St Leonard, St Mary and St John for the colleges. The figures in the upper parts of the flanking lights are the Chosen, who gave up their lives willingly in the service of God. The Burning Bush, the symbol of the Church of Scotland, is contained in the upper part of the window. The scenes at the base depict the Sacrifice of Abraham, the Stoning of St Stephen and the Discovery of Cain's Guilt. Note how the contrasting colours – the red-robed Saviour and the blues and greens of the other characters – draw the eye back to the central figure of Christ.

Flanking this scene are two windows in the style of William Wilson (1905-1972) possibly created by his assistants. The cool tones of these heraldic windows heighten the impact of Webster's Crucifixion. The arms are those of key figures in the College's history. Kennedy's arms are depicted in the left window and those of St Salvator's College in the right.

The five windows on the south wall (left to right)

The memorial window to those lost in the Second World War is also by William Wilson. It was unveiled by Queen Elizabeth (mother of Elizabeth II) in 1950, and symbolises triumph through sacrifice. The central figure is Christ as St Salvator, bearing the wounds of the Crucifixion and the banner of the Resurrection. Left is St Andrew and right, St Leonard with his broken chains. Above these figures are the badges of the Navy, Army and Air Force. The lower panels show Christ Walking on the Waters, the Agony in the Garden and Christ Crowned and Set Amongst the Firmament.

The crucifixion window: central scene

Below this window, in a shrine designed by Hew Lorimer, is the University's Book of Remembrance for those who died in the Second World War.

The window to the right, probably designed by William Wilson but executed by his assistants, depicts Christ Calming the Storm. Note the ark beneath a rainbow, with the dove bringing an olive branch and hope, and the Hand of God blessing a mediaeval galleon in the upper panels. The lower scenes are Jesus's Baptism, Christ as the Shepherd and the Agony in the Garden.

The next two windows are in the Gothic Revival style: both survive from Forbes's refurbishment. The first, by Hardman & Co of Birmingham, commemorates Jessie Playfair, the wife of Hugh Lyon Playfair, who was instrumental in the building's restoration in the 1840s. It depicts Moses and the Burning Bush, Joseph Triumphant in Egypt and Joseph Sold by his Brethren. The second, probably by Ballantine of Edinburgh, is dedicated to Lord Colonsay and depicts Moses and the Ten Commandments, Christ Healing the Sick and the Judgement of Solomon.

The final window before the screen is a memorial to John Campbell Shairp, Principal of the United College 1868-1885, by Henry Holliday (1839-1927), in the Pre-Raphaelite style (right). The female figures represent Virtue (Virtus), Faith (Fides) and Knowledge (Scientia). Below them are the Parable of the Good Samaritan, Christ Preaching in the Temple and Paul Preaching to the Athenian Philosophers.

The windows in the ante-chapel and organ loft

The armorial window in the ante-chapel and the three windows of the organ loft are thought to be by Herbert Hendrie (1887-1947). That in the ante-chapel bears the devices of Alexander Skene, Bishop Kennedy, and Edward Harkness, whose benefaction made possible the 1929-31 refurbishment of the Church. Those in the organ loft cannot readily be seen by the public. The small window to the right of the organ depicts Bishop Kennedy, bearing a book and offering his blessing (see page 7). One of the two larger windows shows figures from the Old Testament, each bearing an instrument: King David with his harp; Jubal, with pan pipes; and Miriam with a tambourine (see page 18). The other depicts the student John Honey, who at risk of his own life rescued five shipwrecked sailors in St Andrews Bay in 1800; the martyrdom of Patrick Hamilton (see page 10); and the Warriors of Righteousness.

Right: Memorial window
to Principal Shairp

The Exterior

$\mathcal{M}$uch of the external decoration of the Church was destroyed at the Reformation. The empty niches give an indication of how many statues must once have adorned the building. However, some interesting features remain.

Opposite the main entrance at the front of the church is an arch, originally part of the college's demolished cloister court, removed in 1761 and erected here in 1906. The area enclosed with railings covers part of the ground which was used as a college cemetery from 1459. The original cemetery wall was removed during Playfair's refurbishment of the college.

In the entrance porch, a central ceiling boss bears Kennedy's arms and a bishop's mitre. The remains of a benatura, or holy-water stoup, can be seen in the north-east corner. The oak doors also bear Kennedy's arms. They are of great age, but not necessarily original.

The niches flanking the eastern bay of the church front bear the arms of Kennedy and James II, his cousin. On the buttress to the left is a sundial, or 'mass clock'.

The tower is the highest-standing building in St Andrews and can be seen from many miles away, contributing to the town's distinctive skyline. Entrance to the college is gained through the pend, or vaulted archway, at the base of the tower. An ornamental panel above the pend bears Kennedy's arms (right). The tower contains a clock, and two bells called Katharine, or 'Kate Kennedy', and Elizabeth. Katharine is the bell of St Salvator's College: legend has it that she was named for the founder's niece. Elizabeth hung in St Leonard's College Church until 1761, when she was brought to St Salvator's. Both bells have been recast several times, most recently in 1940, in tribute to the response of University members in volunteering for service during the Second World War and in hope of a 'righteous peace'.

Bishop Kennedy's Coat of Arms

Further Reading

R G Cant, *The College of St Salvator: Its Foundation and Development including a Selection of Documents*, Edinburgh, 1950.

R G Cant, *St Salvator's Chapel, St Andrews: The College and Collegiate Kirk of St Salvator: A Short Account of the Building and Its History*, St Andrews, 1982.

Abigail Grater, *The United College: The architectural development of the United College of St Salvator and St Leonard, University of St Andrews, 1747-1931*, St Andrews, 2000.

Acknowledgements:

The restoration of the tower and stained glass windows of St Salvator's Chapel from 1999 to 2000 was generously supported by the following trusts, organisations and individuals: Ian Askew Charitable Trust, The Baird Trust, Douglas Charitable Trust, Fife Environment Trust, Gordon Fraser Charitable Trust, Historic Scotland, Manifold Trust, John W McCartney, P F Charitable Trust, The Pilgrim Trust, Scottish Churches Architectural Heritage Trust, A Sinclair Henderson, The Skinners Company Lady Neville Charity, and Miss M E Swinton Paterson's Charitable Trust. Generous gifts were also received from alumni and friends of the University of St Andrews. The clock faces were refurbished with the generous support of Mrs J ' Cookie' R F Matheson in 1999.

Grateful thanks in the preparation of this booklet to: Professor Ian Carradice, Museum Collections; Sarah Fairclough, Museum Collections; Dr Norman H. Reid, Keeper of Manuscripts and Muniments, University Library; William Stevenson, University Organist; Rev Dr James Walker, Chaplain.

Information on worship, preachers, events in the Chapel, and weddings is available on the Chaplaincy website: www.st-andrews.ac.uk/chaplaincy or by contacting: The Chaplaincy, Mansefield, St Mary's Place, St Andrews, Fife, KY16 9UY. Tel: 01334 462866.